Penn F

Poems

Neil Leadbeater

Littoral Press

First published 2019 by:
The Littoral Press, 15 Harwood Place,
Lavenham, Sudbury, Suffolk CO10 9SG

© Neil Leadbeater 2019

ISBN 978-1-912412-17-4

British Library Cataloguing-in-Publication Data:
A catalogue record of this book is available from
The British Library

Cover photograph © Mervyn Linford

Printed and bound in Great Britain by:
4Edge Ltd. Hockley, Essex,
www.4edge.co.uk

For Jane

Acknowledgements:

The author is grateful to the editors of the following publications in which some of these poems, a few in earlier versions, have appeared:

A New Ulster; *Areopagus Magazine*; *As Above So Below*; *CHALLENGER International* (Canada); *Creature Features* (Cyprus); *Dial 174*; *First Literary Review – East* (USA); *Green Silk Journal* (USA); *Jellyfish Whispers* (USA); *Keep Poems Alive*; *Nine Muses Poetry*; *Optimum Poetry*; *Panda Quarterly Poetry Magazine*; *Pennine Ink*; *Phoenix New Life Poetry*; *Poetic Licence*; *Poetry Cornwall*; *Pulsar*; *Quarry*; *Quill & Parchment* (USA); *Reach Poetry*; *Salopeot*; *Sentinel Literary Quarterly*; *The Blackcountryman*; *The Cannon's Mouth*; *The Seventh Quarry*; *The Sound of Poetry Review* (USA); *The Weekly Avocet* (USA); *Time of Singing* (USA); *Urban District Writer* and *Willenhall Life*.

A Midlands Alphabetum was published in the anthology *Best of British* (Paper Swans Press, 2018).

Poem in a Burlap Sack was published in the anthology *Beyond Boundaries* (Liminal Ink, 2018) to complement the Glasgow 2018 European Championships.

Renton Road Allotments is due to appear in the *Long Island Sounds Anthology, 2019 (USA)*.

About the Author:

Neil Leadbeater is an author, essayist, poet and critic living in Edinburgh, Scotland. His short stories, articles and poems have been published widely in anthologies and journals both at home and abroad. His publications include *Hoarding Conkers at Hailes Abbey* (Littoral Press, 2010); *Librettos for the Black Madonna* (White Adder Press, 2011); *The Worcester Fragments* (Original Plus, 2013); *The Loveliest Vein of Our Lives* (Poetry Space, 2014), *Finding the River Horse* (Littoral Press, 2017) and *Punching Cork Stoppers* (Original Plus, 2018). His work has been translated into several languages. He is a regular reviewer for several journals including *Galatea Resurrects (A Poetry Engagement)* (USA); *The Halo Halo Review* (USA); *Contemporary Literary Review India* (India) and *Write Out Loud* (UK).

Contents:

I: Penn Fields

I: Penn Fields

The Firing Line

It was late summer when Mr Pellow introduced us to
the Latin master.

What's the 3rd. person singular, future perfect, of rogo?

He'd click his thumb and second finger,
keep pulling the trigger until we got it right.

Another one:

What's the dative plural of magister?

You could feel the bullet go through you. Five seconds
was all you had. Your concentration was fine-tuned
to such a pitch
that every answer, slammed back,
ricocheted off the racket.

Recite the whole of hic, haec, hoc...

Behind the thick-set glasses, he'd fix us with his stare.
This was his game, his way of driving home
hard facts. Being there was everything.

This urge to break into Latin, to confound
one's opponent, come out on top, made men of us.

Now, ambition attracts.

Me and Wooding, Satchel-light

Me and Wooding, satchel-light,
tumbling home from school.

Feet scambling through Autumn,
the red mulch of copper-beech;
cubs under the moon.

Our beef about detention. The great
unfairness of it, the sheer absurdity
of having to write I MUST NOT
TALK IN CLASS 150 times.

Brown and Mills straggling behind -
voices shrill as sharp-edged knives.

Where have they been all these years,

what have they done with their lives?

Wrottesley Row

Wrottesley Row
was at the far end of the playing field:
a place where a ball
would count for a six.
If you peered through the hedge
you'd see the road
angle away into the middle distance,
close, but out of bounds.

It was the sort of road where you'd expect to see
very expensive houses.
Its name had class. It had a certain
je ne sais quoi. To reach it
you turned right by the notice that read
MINISTRY OF AGRICULTURE,
FISHERIES AND FOOD.

White-flannelled, we'd gather there
and catch some notion of freedom.

To go down the road in an open-topped, racing-green
MG sports car to the streamlined family houses
was our undivided dream.

All that term we thought about it...

It was our paradise.

How did we ever let it go?

A Dazzle of Zebras

When we shook hands with Collective Nouns
this was the one we liked the best
better even than a skulk of foxes
or a bevy of quail
because it made us think of West African antelopes,
zebra finches, referees with striped shirts
in American football and the belisha beacon
at the pedestrian crossing
whose amber flash, after dark,
caught us in its fall.
So it was that Miss Holland sent us out
into the world that day
to be amazed, awed, bedazzled
at the wonder of all we saw.

Summer in the Fast Lane

Seeing the Cropmaster in the open field
Miss Herbert turned from the window.
How do you spell tractor
she asked.
Harry's hand shot up so fast
he was first back with the answer.

Correct, she said.

I, too, could spell that word
but I was too slow to raise my hand.
Even then summer's growth
was quicker than
I thought –

it caught me dreaming in the
Green Corridor
that slow majestic in the minor key
which is

the purple hairstreak lane

the large skipper lane

and the clouded yellow lane

all the things I never wanted
to draw down to a close.

Radstock

Goggle-eyed, you were half way round the racing track
going under
the Meccano bridge by the red Meccano crane.
A soft toy rabbit called Beefy was watching intently
your elder brother
who was busy building a Bayko house in a dream of
London suburbia.
Your mother was ironing tea-towels
because it was Monday and time for Andy Pandy.
The papers were full of the Cold War
but you didn't know about that.
Even then, there was still time to play catch-up…
and waking from sleep in the back of the car
it was only natural to ask aloud
exactly where we were.

A voice from the front said "Radstock".

Springvale

To the rear of Wordsworth Avenue
boys pounding through broomrape
"spikelets oblong or slightly wedge-shaped…
rough towards the tip."

Whatever it is they are running on
the urge to be first at the finishing line
is uppermost in their minds –
it always has been and it always will be
because things like this never change-

the need to succeed is sown.

Poem in a Burlap Sack

Starting is the best.
As I hold the sack waist high
a foot in each corner
for the race ahead
I catch all the odour
from the resin of jute
think of a Kennebec, Kerr
or King Edward -
how Russet Burbanks
make the best hash browns
while others
in a bunch of hops
go for Yukon Gold.

Poem in a Single Leap

This poem is allowed
one leap
so I'll string things out
to cover the distance
as best I can
which means there'll be
a long run into
the storyline -
lots of hyperbole
to fill the gap
in the pit
I never wanted
to land in
but always did
one foot arching for
the furthest jump
I could reach.

Raising the Bar

All those times
I drew myself up
to my full height
and ran like the wind
vaulting over the bar
my mind doing
somersaults
over and over
the crowd going wild
with applause.

Days when the Schools were Closed

We never gave a thought for the levellers,
green-fingered conjurors with heavy-duty boots,
who came in the name of *Grounds Maintenance*
majestic through the gates –
or guessed when the sod-cutters
with their ride-on mowers
would give the pitch a run for its money
top-dressing for games.

Now the posts are up
men are suddenly boys again
playing for extra time.

A Shock to the System

In edgy light you bottled out of the thin copse
heart pounding with the sudden shock
from picking up the can.
"Something shot out of it," you said,
and let your hand rush to your mouth.

"Over there," you said,
"Something's jumping in the grass!"
A pinprick of skin winked in the sun
so we traced its path in the lemon-squash light
until the movement of parting stems
revealed the startled frog.

We leaned over, saw how the fellow
was pop-eyed at rest, the floor of his throat
rising and falling in a gentle, regular rhythm.

It may be a while before he trusts me enough
to stay within this poem.

The Cars we had in our Drive that Day

were the Humber Hawk and Ford Anglia, a green Armstrong
Siddeley, two Morris Oxfords, a Hillman Imp and an Austin
Atlantic Convertible turning in off the Stourbridge Road that
enormous day in June. We all waited while you blew out the
candles -all six in the one breath -with a kiss-me-quick,
mischievous look of glee. After the balloons and after the tea,
the party games when we were fancy free, we watched the cars
slowly leave - a yellow Sunbeam Talbot, a Studebaker Golden
Hawk and two Jaguar Mark X Saloons in blue, silver and grey,
brake lights glowing at the foot of the drive; a raised hand in
salutation waving a last goodbye.

Renton Road Allotments

Renton Road Allotments were on the other side of town
somewhere you'd never been to
but it conjured up the conviviality
of mixing with people from different cultures
who shared a passion for plants -
the Indian amid the still expanse of Exbury hybrid azaleas;
Jamaicans with their summer squashes
huggermugger with massed astilbes
ranged between the beans
and a small child
bad-mouthing belladonna
because his father had told him
it was the only fruit in the town grounds
of which he could not eat.

Frederick Street

was the axis of all things electrical -
old wind-up gramophones,
the home of broadcaster sapphire needles
that would play
The Laughing Policeman
5,000 times without replacement
priced six shillings and sixpence
(tax paid).

Days like this we'd cross the street
headed for the baths.
The air was electric. Sparks flew
with the thrill of who could do the crawl
or dive from the highest board.

Knowing where we were going
we felt the hum of danger
singing down the wires -
it broke inside us like sheet lightning
and lit us up for miles.

Photographing West Park

Picture this:

His big idea
was to capture the park -
to pin it down on film.
So he framed all he could
of the "hungry leas"
that span of land between
Park Road East and Park Road West;
snapped up yards,
borders, piers;
and the figures of youths
round carousels
caught like moths
in amber.

Memorandum to the Board of the
Villiers Engineering Company

Pedaling fast down Marston Road
for lemonade and crisps
I passed the gates of your factory once,
aged six.
I never knew you'd make the parts
for all the bikes I'd own...
I had to catch up
on all the fun
which was choosing the crisps
at the corner shop
and taking the pop
back home.

A Midlands Alphabetum

Abercrombie Street.
Builders' merchants
Clocking-on.
Daybreak cracks them open; it sandbags them into
Elemental labour while next door's
Foundry fires a slab of
Galvanized iron into a
Hot-rolled metal bar. The sum of their lives
Inches off the production line. It makes them
Jump the queue at the works canteen for a
Kit-Kat snack on the hoof. Across the street a
Lone operative smokes away her well-earned break while a
Manufacturer of scrap compaction
Number-crunches the working day into a state of abject
Oblivion. Wesley's
Pressworks padlocked-off.
Quiet nights
Rolling down like Venetian blinds on the
Storm water attenuation tanks; keys
Turning in back doors. Lighting-
Up time. The night shift cascading into focus.
Voices off. A boxful of
Widgets, plugs and spigots, the
Xerox copier shuttling sheets back and forth like
Ying and yang or the strung string of the Yo-yo, the spark of
Zinc in the zero-hour; dark glass after midnight.

Outstanding Natural Beauty

Off Worcester Street
this building with the roof blown off
is a shell of its former storey
but inside
-if you can call it that-
the cabbage whites
on the purple buddleia
are the life and soul of the party.

Shock Absorbers: A Poem in Five Relays

Every minute he strikes the ground
180 times.

Trees along the boundary edge.
The trees at ease. The trees easy.

Scarlet runners high on their poles
a blur in the old allotments.

Cross-country in rough weather
the shock of punctured ground.

My father running in Dartmouth Park
a week before the war.

Hope Street

My grandparents lived in a street called Hope,
in the back-to-back red marl brick
that was in earshot of Albion playing at home.
They were a good match.

Long after they had gone, I walked through the
downstairs rooms. In the dream,
it was just as they had left them. The back door
was still off the latch, the mangle
in the scullery, the piano by the wall.
The holidays in Rhyl were still in their frames.
Each faded photograph a memory
I had no part of; it was like the glassworks
that I never saw but heard about through talk:
the bottles he fired for sauce.

On the table was his business card and in that
moment I wanted to dial Willenhall 89
on the black Bakelite telephone
that rested in the hall. It was the number for
the bottle factory, Toll End, Tipton, Staffs.

Why do we always leave it too late
to ever make that call?

Willenhall Locks

Every latch tells a story -
doors open into old interiors,
people whose lives
have been lockfast for years.
Here at the Lock Museum
we learn about locksmiths,
makers of spurs,
producers of latch cams,
bolts and keys,
instruments for turning,
winding, tuning -
everything from a wooden wedge
to a tapered piece of metal
for fixing the boss of a wheel -
how each master
would make his tools:
chisels, screwdrivers,
saws and drills -
an assemblage of skills
mutually engaged
before the factories
hit the big time
with names like Yale and Parkes.

Ann Street

In Willenhall, the "Winehale" of Domesday,
synonymous with locks,
slum rubble, bulldozed to death,
circumscribed the street.

When the factory came
a great Goliath of moving works ground out its parts.

I remember the weight of the tonnage,
the constant hum of presses,
pallet boxes for the finished goods,
and the power-driven trucks that moved them round
routinely to the bay.
Overhead, a light-weight crane, controlled by suspended
push-button switches, handled the heavier gear.
My father showed me the nuts and bolts
jumbled in the coop.
I dipped my hand to scoop the slack, and marvelled
as it showered back,
a black mass of gleaming grit
heaving in the dark.

Dudley Port

A port ……..at Dudley?

But port business went on here
in lieu of a flight of locks.
The Venice of the Midlands
was awash with canals:
barge traffic for Birmingham.

After that, the railways came:
great tracks of parallel lines
shunting through the backs.
Six depots and seven stations
fought at the buffers for
Bilston steel, freight-loads
of glass, Willenhall locks.

Vocabularies for the Jewellery Trade

Breaking in was easy. The window locks
had rusted off and half the panes
were missing. Inside
we slogged like laggards through the lemel
and grabbed all the tools we could find:
collet blocks, bezel pushers, bick iron, drills;
our pockets bulged with binding wire
and a slew of pan-head screws.

And we ran and we ran, man to man,
the sirens ringing like steel shot
as we swung right over the wall...

-a bellyful of burrs, pin-chucks, tweezers -
the swag like blood on our hands all day
and not a jewel between us.

Leaving New Street

Beyond the tunnels there were factories and cranes, a compendium
of car parks, junk yards, tips; bulldozers shifting history.
Tower blocks bestrode the landscape. The Monday wash,
draped over railings, dried in the midday heat.

Along the way, a series of signs in quick succession
told us where we were at: *Smethwick Rolfe Street - Smethwick
Rolfe Street - Smethwick Rolfe Street -*

The summer haze, airless and venal,
congealed with the log-jam of trade:
foundries, lighting and switchgear; dossils, plugs and valves;
they put back in place all those things
that I thought I had nearly lost:
the smell of malt from a Midlands brewery,
the red marl of the back-to-backs; a school bell in a comprehensive
ringing me back to Maths.

I lived here once, much as I lived in other towns
but none has brought me back so much as this -
nosing the scent of something gone,
the past we always miss.

The Progress of Cattle Newly Escaped into Staffordshire

Three bullocks and six heifers, red-roan bay to dark plum brindle, careered in sequence, helter-skelter, down the left-hand lane of the A51 to the dense veil of Hopwas Woods. Cars braked, having no choice, swerving to curb disaster. Now the subject of a POLICE ALERT, a lead article already warns that the *Tamworth Nine have escaped the catch of soldiers.* The extent of their freedom thrills and frightens them. Loutish, edgy and semi-feral, they are out of the bounds of their minds.

Repton Fields

i

In the Fives Court
the gloved argument of harsh words
bouncing off the wall.

ii

Ringing the changes
between French and Maths:
the school bell.

iii

With military precision
the Latin master strategically disarms
Caesar's Gallic Wars.

iv

After the blessing of God Almighty
the organist in his black gown
pulls out all the stops.

v

Seconds after the big hit
a ball enters the long grass
and rolls up to its rest.

vi

The only Greek
I ever came home with:
alpha beta +.

Willow

At Willington, in the hundred of Morleston
and Litchurch,
there are willows that grow aslant a brook
on the flood plain of the Trent. I went there once
to watch their slender, pliant branches
weep for Ophelia
but there were no crowflowers or long purples,
just a stretch of fishermen angling for a catch.
I must have been there for an hour or more
thinking about the slantwise willows
the way they were dreaming of ox-bow rivers –
facts out of geography I'd stored for later
to put in my school exam.
                              There were
reeds there and cow parsley
whose tops were holed like kitchen colanders
face upturned to the sun
but my mind abounded in willows
for it was the willows that I had come to see
that hot afternoon when I baled out of school
and no-one knew where I'd gone.

Buying Apples from Mr. Aldridge

Buying apples from Mr Aldridge was easy in the 'fifties -
dessert or culinary,
you simply took whatever he had: a Cox's Orange Pippin
or a heavy cropping Bramley Seedling -
there was not much else to choose from –
no D'Arcy Spice or Laxton's Fortune;
nothing fancy then.

I'd watch him place the black weights
squarely on the scale.

For a brief moment he'd hold the hoard of orchards
sunlit from the pail.

His smile was the seal on our purchase.
It weighed in his favour. It was the kind of courtesy
that was made for business. The look that
sent out a signal that he'd go that extra mile.

Everywhere I went I learnt to keep that smile.

Not Raving but Clowning

Stevie, I too loved Grovelands Park.

I was sailing my boat on the lake
when you were sitting
on the opposite bank
bringing a poem to life.
I was shouting then in boyish glee
gesticulating, as children do,
not raving but clowning.

II: Wolverhampton Locks

Wolverhampton Locks

Lock 1

Chubb on my mind all day.

Years back,
this red brick building
distinct, undulled,
thrummed with the
noise of trade.

I hold up my hands
a little apart to get
the long perspective:
the lock framed
by fingers and thumbs –
the span of its definition.

Lock 2

Coins slip from my hand.
One rolls so close
to the edge
that I hold my breath
at the hapless thought of it
falling into the pound.

Lock 3

What I remember is this:
a man hitting the ground running.

I wonder for a second
where he has come from
and where he is going to
and then dismiss him
on a count of ten
clean out of my mind.

Lock 4

Rain thumbing the brickwork.
Brewer's building, Victorian listed,
gutted once by fire.

The boatmen opening paddles
much as a barman
would pull a pint
watching the beer fill the glass
up to the level mark.

Lock 5

Beating the barge traffic
hands down
the dog runs on
impetuous as ever
the fastest thing
on legs.

Lock 9

I look into the lock
but the water is stubborn
and will not yield.

No words will come today.

Lock 12

On bad weather days
this is our turning point –
something understood
between a man, a dog
and a viaduct. Obedient,
the dog bounds off
but he's not chasing
pentameters. His paws are
in much too much of a hurry
to take account of metre.

Lock 13

Briefly, we mark time
until the 10.35
has worked its way
out of Wolverhampton
northbound for Crewe.

When I look into water
I look into sky.
How everything shimmers
upside down –
trees, buildings, people, birds –
a child's small balloon.

Lock 14

A barge is about to enter.
As the sluice opens
I study the water
gushing with intention.

Gnats roil in the heat.

It will be fine weather
tomorrow.

Lock 15

In the watershed of England
a night of soaking rain.

Orange hawkweed
bent double

stems fractured by storms.

Lock 17

Far from the centre,
all that nests in the soft down
is the sedge warbler
content to have found
the perfect haunt in the reedbed.
I recognize its dark brown back
and dusky legs
the distinctive stroke
above each eye
milk-white on the colour chart
as I stop on the towpath
to listen to its song –
not so much an
attenuated churring
but more a kind of bird chatter
on the arable edge of town.

Lock 19

How everything thins to this:

the old husk of the city gone.

The dog dashes
after thrown sticks

his dog day begun.

Lock 21

Bottom lock. John Brown's
toll house long since gone.

Beside the racecourse
horsepower and engine power
jockey for position.

A woodpigeon clears its throat.

III: A Short Walk on the Long Mynd

A Short Walk on the Long Mynd

That short walk on the Long Mynd
was a long haul through history.
We were catching up on ages past through
Broadhill Dale and Burnell's Brook;
Gogbatch and Grindle Hollow;
bracken-high and heather-sprung
with our staunch Quaker grit.

Later, on the steep descent
We were hind's feet in high places
with Habbakuk still in our Sunday heads.
The sky-blown wings of the rare ring ouzel
soared into the blue
and Cardingmill Valley lay far below
the road no bigger than ribbon strips

the six of us and you.

Poem for the Stiperstones

Years back it was the constant freezing and thawing -
the tight grip and the slow release -
that relaxed you. It shattered your quartzite
into jumbled scree and left your jagged outcrops
a rubble-strewn ridge of rough-edged tors
defiant in the black.

They called you the neglected mountain -
a cold appendage of the Long Mynd -
the heavy sulk of the hard done by
who wants to be left alone. But
"Back to Purple" in your grey escarpments
is giving you the edge -
the appeasement of a hard exterior
slowly gaining ground.

Clee Hill

"Clee, how you cleave the wind!"

-Richard Wheeler: Remembering Summer.

Clee, you follow us far and near, there is no hiding
your profile, you are the hog-back
that lies astride the meeting-point of rocks
that vast explosion of volcanic filaments
that earned you a mark of distinction
among the laundered landscape -
a patchwork quilt of farms and fields
squeezed out of the wringer.

Objects at Upper Ludstone

This winter-serviced and well-sharpened machinery
standing idle in a farmer's yard
draws me in -
it's more to do with colour
than anything mechanical -
red is a statement I like a lot
it makes me wait
for inspiration

until the green light comes.

Claverley

It's the steep descent into Claverley
that thrills me most
the way those high sandstone banks
bound the curvature
of the narrow lane
and the sudden leap
of the heart to the mouth
when a vehicle coming
the other way
throws us into reverse.

Wrekin

Between the wild Shropshire hills
and the flat northern lands
this whale-back hump
on Severn Plain
wind and rain rounding it down
to the nearest decimal point.

Ratlinghope

Ratlinghope - a name that takes you unawares
like a catch in the back of the throat.
In Domesday it was Rotelinghope, a manor of two hides,
and latterly Ratchup
-a version possibly created by the post office
but no-one knows for sure-
so much to say about the name alone
the place itself so small.

Loveliest of Trees

Blossom caught our attention.
How could we miss it –
large or small, single or double,
Noyes' "seas of bloom" –
confetti that never ceased to bring
joy from the marriage of
beauty observed and words
keenly drawn:
a swirl of raspberry
and whipped cream
delicate as cupcakes
crumbly as scones
or a thin coating of sieved flour
dusting a luscious sponge.

IV: Sheep in Twin-Sets

Sheep in Twin-Sets

Set I

The Cheviot

The collie rounds them up
for the group photograph –
half a hirsel in a
No Through Road near Kelso.
We funnel them into the lens,
view the wool behind the ears,
the thick fleece, replete enough,
for a little warmth in the heart.

The White Face Dartmoor

Winter is the white face of Dartmoor.
Snow soft as lambswool
carpeting the twisted oaks
in Wistman's Wood
where sheep have strayed
from meagre pasture
to graze among the tangled roots
of ancient trees
whose collective constitution
has now outlived all ends.

The Dartmoor

Buried under drifts of snow
you still emerge unharmed.
How you do this
no one knows.
It is your vanishing-point,
the party trick
you play the most
whenever the weather
gets cold.

The Blackface

After the shearing
you are the soft filling
in a king-sized mattress
on which the rich
lie on their backs
counting themselves
to sleep.

The Black Welsh Mountain

Blah blah black sheep
bleating on about
nothing in particular:

three bags full.

The Derbyshire Gritstone

Grazing in the Pennines
do you ever think of those
dark satanic mills –
of Hebden Bridge and Halifax,
of spinning jennies and
Jacquard looms,
of the roar of manufactuary,
the incomparable quality
of a Masham wool
with a lustrous sheen
machine washable
for easy care?

Yes | No | Possibly.

The Whiteface Woodland

Rare but not endangered
you once grazed the high peak
where three counties meet
inhospitable in Glossop land.
Sheep of the heavy snowfall,
of the wind-whipped waterlogged bogs,
indifferent to the intrusion
of intrepid ramblers in sodden cagoules
getting the measure
of Pennine weather
with poles to mark the way.

Set II

The Swaledale

Lodged in the spine of England
between the Tyne Gap
and the High Pennines
lie the Swaledales.
Their loose fleece is familiar
as field barns
and their ram's horns
swept back behind the ears
are a gesture of defiance.
They are like throwaway commas
which tell the reader
there is more to come
before the end of the story.

The Scotch Blackface

These are "the Blackies"
on black heather hills
resilient in all weathers,
not at all sheepish
but Galloway types
frustrating the flockmaster's
collie's plans
to herd them at the first whistle
with woolly thoughts
of their own.

The Jacob

Always a flock, a hurtle or a mob
never a sounder, a leap or a pride –
each to its own unique descriptor –
the sportings of nature
speckled and spotted
ever since time began.
Some say you have something of
the Middle East in you,
that you are dyed-in-the-wool
Mesopotamian,
more Jacob than Laban
or more Laban than Jacob
and of indeterminate colour:
ringstraked lambs
wanting to belong
to one or the other
but in reality both.

The Hexham Leicester

I imagine you standing
among scabbled stones
surrounded by ramparts
five feet thick
rubbing your flank
on quartzose grit
backside to the wind.

The Lincoln Longwool

You find them in unexpected places –
a pouch-full in Australia, hollows in
New Zealand, Patagonian
prairie pockets…
all of them a far cry
from the bells of Lincoln cathedral
but sound can travel
a long distance…
you only have to hear
the tintinnabulations of sheep bells
to judge by the jingle
how near and far
they are.

The Herdwick

has the homing instinct.
Boomerang sheep that will watch a gate
night and day
as the chief means of escape
or butt a wall at louping height
to find the weakest point
for that single-minded side-roll
to hoof it back to the heaf.

Postscript: A Poem worth its Weight in Wool

The time I took Jenny for a spin
one foot on the treadle
I could have sworn a part of her
unraveled a memory
which had weighed on her mind
since birth:

7 lbs = 1 clove
2 cloves = 1 stone
2 stones = 1 tod
6½ tods = 1 wey
2 weys = 1 sack
12 sacks = 1 last…

The accumulation of profit
shorn from her body
shear after shear.

V: Blue Anchor

The Rollright Stones

How far did they roll to get here,
or were they just here anyway?
Suppose they had rolled right into position
or gone the wrong way
needing to be coaxed
back on track –
maybe they were destined
to go right instead of left
because of the weight inside them
but what if they had rolled
off-centre?
That might be the subject
of a further poem.

All the King's Men

In the shoulder of Oxfordshire
Burl's lumps of leprous limestone
famously uncountable
circle the field:
Humpty Dumpty stones
'corroded,' according to Stukeley,
'like worm-eaten wood
by the harsh jaws of Time' –
a funerary monument
guarding bones
which the living visit daily
to understand the past.

Round-headed Rampions

I like the sound of them, their six syllable music –
how they make a song and dance
for short poems like these –
so here they are, chalk champions on leafless stems
a midsummer marriage of flower and field
purple haze on Malling Down
the pride of Shelley's Sussex.

Yellow Waxbells

are not hollow vessels
struck by a clapper
but Corninthian capitals
in Xanthus
whose flared mouths
sport shuttlecock blooms
the colour of egg yolk,
primrose or lemon –
day beauties
who bow their heads
as if sound could
yet come out of them.

Leopard's Bane

Impossible to miss you
-*total yellow* –
like corn marigold or chamomile:
a warm-up after winter.
You are the spotted wildcat
in the Spring border
but there is nothing catlike about you.
All the animal in you
has gone to ground:
those subterranean runners
escaping into the wild.

Bryony

Could be a girl's name –
someone fresh out of school at four
on the shortest distance to run.
May to June we see her
sprinting through cleavers, brambles, scrub
in a green uniform with red berries
satchel flying with linear programming
still in her bright young head.

Black Bryony

Like honeysuckle and hops you are Lady's Seal,
looping through a length of hedge
with your Ace of Spades blades -
Clare's 'scallop'd bryony,'
that twists in a set direction
with the forward motion of clocks.
Chasing time, you scramble
through brambles, goosegrass, bindweed
conspicuous in your autumn dress
when summer has gone to bed.

Poem for the Lesser Celandine

You are the flower that lines the fields
diminutive yellow: Lawrence's
"scalloped splashes of gold"
poisonous if ingested raw –
America's noxious weed –
growing when the days are short
asleep by the end of May.

Hedgehog

No one could call you spineless.
The armour takes care of that.
Getting to the heart of you is hard –
that quiet determination that lets you
get on with living...
Sight failing in half-light
we hear you in hedgerows
scavenging for slugs –
watch you curl into a defensive ball
just like you do in your hibernation
when breathing almost stops.

Selling Elvers in the Close Season

is hard, especially if a water bailiff
from the Severn Fishery Board is
out to catch you slip-handed
at the end of April 1904.
So let's change the letters round
because you can sell *levers* any time.
They can open up a can of worms
just like a ring pull
can rip the band aid off a pint of lager
no questions asked.
Everyone likes a sliver of gossip
with a drink to wash it down
even the court at the Petty Sessions
who fined the hawker five shillings
and seven more for costs.

Tidal

Extraordinary what a river can do
in a major storm to cricket,
especially if it's the Severn
at Gloucester
on a rough day in January, 1930
when the pavilion floated
on Castle Meadow,
spilling out its innards –
bats, pads, gloves and stumps,
the paint used for white-lining
all bowled out lbw
loosed by water
led astray.

The Fire at Gloucester Docks, 1907

The irony of fire near water,
how it took hold
snubbing everything
while the dock lay placid
in its liquid depth,
its deep-sea thinking,
undisturbed, unconcerned,
unmoved.

Samuel Bowley's Final Ride through the Civic Streets of Gloucester

Friends turned up in their hundreds. Had he been alive
it would have been to wish him Happy Birthday
instead it was Many Happy Returns
to Heaven. For he had come full circle
from the Quaker School in Nailsworth to this last
can't-put-a-foot-wrong formality. Shunning hymns,
he would have played down praise
raised in his honour, would have appreciated
the quiet respect shown by the masses,
the pubs that were shut
against the evils of drink
as the hearse passed their doors
stone sober.

Bank Holiday Monday in Longford Park, 1881

People came from as far afield as Cardiff,
Hereford, Swindon, to trek through
the hub of Gloucester
out to Longford Park -
a green thought in a green shade
that Mr Robinson had opened up
for an afternoon of dancing.
His lawns had seen nothing like it,
all that fancy footwork
in the Blue Danube waltzing,
and then the debris of spent rockets
whose fizz had gone to ground.

As You Like It

Although the building work at the Theatre Royal
was not yet complete
the performance went ahead on the understanding
that the plasterwork would be done later.
Critics said it was rough at the edges,
uneven, even,
but the raw quality added a layer
not seen before.

Blue Anchor

In the hip-joint of Somerset, this ball and socket Bay.

The name conjures up shipping, especially when lowered
or lifted up
its surface glistening with sunlit molluscs
dredged up from the deep.

If you follow the tides
you can catch the moment they are on the turn
that brief breathing-while of indecision
when they come so far and go no further
like guests who discover
that it's time to leave
so as not to outstay a welcome

as you do, Nautilus, every day,
taking your cue from the moon.

The Thriplow Daffodils

They are Europe's floral headdress. Asphodels in Elysian fields. Traps for Persephone. Opening up on Ash Wednesday and dying back at the end of Lent to a round underground bulb. Flowers conspicuous by corona trumpets, bell-shaped, bowl-shaped daffa-down dillies with linear, strap-shaped leaves.

Paper-white jonquils in figure-of-eight lanes that haste away too soon; that die of their own dear loveliness; that are full-throated and bid the year be bold. Incredible seas of white and yellow having the time of their lives.

Shelley throwing caution to the wind.

Walking on Sunshine

Treading on that solar flare
scorched you with
so much happiness –
it burnt itself into you
all day long
on the dance floor
of the world.

Notes on the Poems

The title of this collection refers to the name of a local area of Wolverhampton where I was born and grew up. It is largely residential with a variety of housing stock ranging from modest terraced homes to large detached residences. At some stage in the distant past, being a mile or so south west from the centre, it would have been fields which is why a large part of the area, in recognition of its former farming lands, is still known today as Penn Fields.

Photographing West Park

The site chosen for the first of the large parks in Wolverhampton was the Race Course, or Broad Meadows, owned by the Duke of Cleveland. On 12 March 1879, Alderman Samuel Dickonson, invited landscape gardeners to compete for the layout of the park. The winner of the £50 prize was Richard Hartland Vertegans of Chad Valley Nurseries, Edgbaston, Birmingham. The park was opened on 6 June 1881.

Wolverhampton Locks

The locks in this sequence refer to the 21 numbered locks along the Birmingham Main Line Canal from Broad Street Basin in the centre of Wolverhampton to Aldersley Junction.

In **Lock 1**, "Chubb" is a reference to the Chubb building, originally built in 1898-9, to house the headquarters of the Chubb Lock and Safe manufactory, one of Wolverhampton's major industries. It is now a Grade II-listed Victorian warehouse that has been converted to house a centre for the creative arts.

In **Lock 13** the word "balloon" is a reference to the series of balloon flights flying on coal gas that took place at the gas works nearby. On 5 September 1862 the world record for a balloon ascent without oxygen was set by balloonists taking off from here. The balloon, flying on coal gas, reached 37,000 feet - a record that still stands. During the two and a half hour flight, scientist James Glaisher passed out and balloonist Henry Coxwell only managed to save the day by pulling on the balloon's ripcord with his teeth after he lost the use of his hands. For more information see *Black Country Ramblings: Along the Old Main Line, Part 2* by P. Clayton (*The Blackcountryman* Autumn 2017. Vol.50 No.4 pp58-62).

Sheep in Twin-Sets

Counting Sheep by Philip Walling (Profile Books, 2014) and *British Sheep and Wool* edited by J. B. Skinner, D. E. Lord and J.M. Williams (The British Wool Marketing Board, 1985) provided source material for this sequence of poems.

The Rollright Stones and **All The King's Men**

The Rollright Stones is a complex of three Neolithic and Bronze Age megalithic monuments near the village of Long Compton, on the borders of Oxfordshire and Warwickshire. One of these monuments is known as the King's Men stone circle.

Samuel Bowley's Final Ride through the Civic Streets of Gloucester

Samuel Bowley (1802-1884) was a Quaker philanthropist, an anti-slavery and temperance campaigner and a past president of the National Temperance League. During his youth he had a sound business training under his father. In 1829 he started up in business as a cheese factor in Gloucester. He became chairman of many local banking, gas, railway, and other companies, and for the last twenty years of his life he was looked upon as a leader in commercial circles and affairs. He died in Gloucester on Sunday, 28 March 1884, the eighty-second anniversary of his birthday. A huge number of people, both rich and poor, attended his funeral.

Walking on Sunshine

The title of this poem is taken from the song title sung by Katrina and the Waves.